SHATTERED STREETS, SILENT CRIES

By SRB De'POET
(SRB)

Published By
SRB DE'POET
and
Tia Shonae Williams

_____

"In Memory of my sister,

Joan McGregor"

"Losing my sister to cancer left a silence in my heart that words can never fill, but her love, her laughter, and her strength live on in every breath I take."

By: SRB De'POET

SHATTERED STREETS, SILENT CRIES

Copyright © 2025

SRB De'POET™

The Inspiration Behind "Shattered Streets, Silent Cries"
By: SRB De Poet.

"Shattered Streets, Silent Cries" was born out of a profound sense of duty to give a voice to the overlooked and forgotten in British society. SRB De'POET was deeply moved by the growing inequalities and injustices that plague the United Kingdom. Witnessing the struggles of the elderly, veterans, and marginalised groups sparked an emotional response that he skilfully wove into his poetry. The book is both a reflection and a call to action, challenging readers to confront these issues with empathy and resolve.

One of the key inspirations for the book was the plight of war veterans who have been abandoned by the very country they once risked their lives to protect. SRB De'POET's experiences and conversations with veterans revealed their heartbreaking struggles with homelessness, mental health, and the lack of adequate support systems. These stories fuelled his desire to amplify their voices, using his poetry as a medium to shed light on their sacrifice and suffering.

Similarly, the neglect faced by the elderly in modern Britain served as a cornerstone for SRB De' POET's creative journey. Many elderly individuals, who once contributed to building the nation, now live in isolation, deprived of care and companionship. This societal indifference resonated deeply with SRB De'POET, who felt compelled to advocate for their dignity and well-being through his heartfelt verses.

The surge in criminal activities and the erosion of community values also provided a stark backdrop for "Shattered Streets, Silent Cries". SRB De'POET observed how fear and mistrust have taken root in neighbourhoods once characterised by unity and safety. His poetry captures this disheartening transformation, urging society to restore a sense of security and solidarity that has been lost.

Personal experiences and encounters played a significant role in shaping the themes of the book. SRB De'POET's experience in his past roles gave him a unique perspective on societal breakdown. From safeguarding lives to witnessing firsthand the struggles of vulnerable populations, these experiences lent authenticity and urgency to his poetic expressions.

The title "Shattered Streets, Silent Cries" encapsulates the essence of the book: a nation fractured by indifference yet brimming with unheard voices yearning for change. SRB

De'POET's powerful imagery and evocative language compel readers to confront uncomfortable truths and consider their role in fostering a more compassionate society.

Ultimately, the inspiration behind "Shattered Streets, Silent Cries" is rooted in SRB De'POET's unwavering belief in humanity's potential for redemption. By highlighting the struggles of the forgotten and the voiceless, he seeks to ignite a collective consciousness, urging society to rebuild itself with compassion, respect, and justice at its core.

All Rights Reserved

No part of this book may be reproduced in any form,
by photocopying or by any electronic or mechanical means,
including information storage or retrieval systems,
without permission in writing from both the copyright
owner and the publisher of this book.
SRB De'POET and Tia Shonae Williams

Shattered Streets, Silent Cries

by SRB De'POET

ISBN:

978-1-0369-2108-8

Publication Date:

July 2025

Publisher:

Independent Publishing Network

T Williams / SRB De'POET

ISBN: 978-1-0369-2108-8

Author: SRB De'POET

Website:

www.srbdepoet.com

Email: srbthepoet@gmail.com

July 2025

SHATTERED STREETS, SILENT CRIES

by

SRB De'POET

S Blackwell

Printed in

Great Britain

www.srbdepoet.com

Message of Recognition

I extend my heartfelt gratitude to the exceptional individuals who contributed their time, talent, and unwavering support towards the creation of this book.

T Williams
Both your insightful perspectives and thoughtful input added depth and clarity to this work. Your contributions helped shape its purpose and direction.
Your constructive feedback played a pivotal role in enhancing the book's overall message. Your support has been invaluable.

D Bromfield
Your dedication and keen attention to detail strengthened the quality of this project. Your commitment is truly appreciated.

G Thompson
Your guidance, encouragement, and shared wisdom provided crucial support throughout this journey.

O Anderson
This book would not have been possible without your collective efforts and belief in its vision. Thank you for being an integral part of this literary endeavour.

With deepest gratitude,
SRB De'POET
(SRB)

Acknowledgements & Thank You

This book would not have been possible without the unwavering love, strength, and encouragement of those closest to me. I am humbled and forever grateful.

To My Family:
Mum and Stepdad – your guidance and support have been the bedrock of my journey.

Stacey-Ann, Georgie, Millie, Tia, Alano, Ayana, and Dawn, thank you for being my anchor.
Shantel, Theo, Rosemary, Chevar, Rohan, Janiel, Sanya, Shaoline, Nova, Jayren and Boyke – each of you has touched my life in ways that words cannot fully express. Your love, laughter, and presence inspire me daily.

To My Friends:
Ash, Raza, Gregory Harris, Gary White, Richard, Noel, Miah, Brimie, James, Billel, Omar Anderson, Andy Sinclair, Khori Hyde, Lennox (Freddy) Anglin, Romeo Hyde, Gary Barnet, Hem Gamit, Richard Johnson, Radcliffe Johnson, Derrick Newby, – thank you for believing in me, challenging me, and walking this path with me. Your friendship has been a constant source of strength and motivation.

This book is not only a reflection of my voice, but a tribute to the many lives, conversations, memories, and love that have shaped it. Thank you for standing by me.

With deep appreciation,
SRB De'POET

ABOUT THE AUTHOR

SRB DE' POET, discovered his passion for poetry at the tender age of ten. Rooted in a deep connection to his rich cultural heritage and life's often harsh realities, SRB De'POET voice emerged early as one both observant and bold. Over the years, his craft evolved into a powerful medium for storytelling, one that captures the pain, pride, and perseverance of everyday people. His poetry dives into the complexities of history, social injustice, and the raw emotional terrain of human experience, creating verses that resonate deeply with readers from all walks of life.

As the author of the compelling book "Shattered Streets, Silent Cries", SRB De'POET brings attention to those often overlooked, society's forgotten souls, the mentally ill, the impoverished, elderly, and homeless veterans. His words serve not just as artistic expression, but as a form of advocacy, illuminating the voices of the unheard and honoring unsung heroes. A creative force and visionary, SRB DE' POET uses his gift to inspire hope, awaken conscience, and call for unity and compassion in a fractured world.

TABLE OF CONTENTS

ABOUT THE AUTHOR 7
1 Life's Echoes 10
2 Money is Not the Root of All Evil 11
3 The Man of the Street 12
4 I am Sorry 13
5 Lost to the Streets 14
6 The Silent Struggles: A Verse on Mental Health 15
7 Death on Our Street 17
8 No Winners 18
9 United We Stand Against Knife Crime 19
10 Why Do We Do the Things We Do? 20
11 Blood on the Streets of London 21
12 Lost Generation 22
13 Shattered Streets 23
14 Silent Cries 24
15 The Street Speaks 25
16 Hidden Scars 26
17 Forty Years of Pain 28
18 Rise Above 29
19 Never Give Up 30
20 Child Abuse Knows No Boundaries 31
21 What Kind of World? 32
22 Our Children 33
23 Freedom of Speech 34
24 No Hopes, No Dream 35
25 Silent Steps 36
26 Having Seeds of Hope 37
27 A Child's Truth 38
28 The Power Within 39
29 Never Let the Street Think for You 40
30 Forgotten Soldiers 41

31 Word is Power 42

32 Rise Above 43

33 I Will Decide My Own Destiny 44

34 Letting Go 45

35 9/11 46

36 Shattered Streets, Silent Fears 47

37 Youth Poverty, a Cry for Help 48

38 Kindness 49

39 Our Heroes Live 50

40 Justice Unyielding 51

41 Where Are They Now? 52

42 Think Before You Act 54

43 God is the Anchor 55

44 What More Can You Take? 56

45 Would You Treat Me the Same? 57

46 Bridging the Gap 58

47 United We Stand to Save Our Youths 60

48 If We Fail Them Today 61

49 The Light We Pass On 62

50 Where is Our Greatness? 63

51 Our Everyday Heroes 64

52 The Weight He Bears 66

1

Life's Echoes

When a baby is born,
We lift them like heroes,
As if arrival alone
Were a deed worth immortal praise.

But when someone departs,
We cover their faces,
As if death itself
Were a secret to erase.

What should bring us shame,
Are the deeds left undone,
The cruelty, the silence,
The shadows we shun.

Life is a breath,
A flicker, a flame,
Not the start or the finish
But how we play the game.

We cry "Ah!" at birth,
In awe of fresh light,
And whisper it softly
When day fades to night.

Between those two sighs
Lies all that we are,
Dreams, wounds, and wonders,
Our stories' scar.

After death, we rise.
Unfettered, untamed,
Judged not by the ending,
But by how we were named.

2

Money is Not the Root of All Evil

They led us to think,
Money is the root of all evil,
But it's not.
It's the hunger for power, unchecked greed,
The fear of not having enough to feed,
The dreams we fought for, yet forgot.

Lack of education is the root of all evil,
A mind left barren, potential suppressed.
Ignorance breeds hate, fuels despair,
Leaving broken souls gasping for air,
A world where wisdom is oppressed.

Lack of opportunity is the root of all evil,
Doors sealed shut before hope can rise.
Ambitions stifled, talent ignored,
Promises shattered, futures floored,
Hope fades as destiny dies.

Injustice is the root of all evil,
When fairness bows to selfish gain.
When laws protect the powerful few,
And the weak have no refuge in view,
This breeds anger, sorrow, and pain.

Corruption is the root of all evil,
Hearts twisted by deceitful hands.
A world where morals lose their light,
Where wrong prevails over what's right,
And honesty barely stands.

So, blame not money but the souls that stray,
Who choose greed over love and give hate its sway.
Money's a tool, neither good nor vile,
But how it's used can build or defile,
Creating worlds of peace or decay.

3

The Man of the Street

I wanted to be the man of the street,
Making dough, stacking bread, living elite.
Surrounded by friends, all chasing the dream,
Blind to the cost, caught up in the scheme.

Didn't care who got hurt in my quest,
Who fell behind or faced eternal rest.
Chasing the thrill, fast money, and fame,
Never considered the cost of the game.

But luck ran dry; the cops closed in,
Caught in the web of my reckless sin.
Shackled in chains, my freedom stripped,
Reality hit, my life's script flipped.

Where are my friends in this darkest hour?
Gone like the wind, lost to the power.
Family burdened by shame and tears,
Left to face my regrets and fears.

Pressure mounts, and hope fades fast,
Memories haunt from a shattered past.
Too late now to rewind the clock,
Trapped behind bars, locked in a box.

If only I'd seen what this life would cost,
Maybe I wouldn't be paying this loss.
But hindsight's cruel, and lessons come late,
A path once chosen now sealed by fate.

4

I am Sorry

I am sorry, Mother, I am sorry, Father,
I chased the thrill; I chose the strife.
Blind to love, deaf to reason,
I gambled with fate and lost my life.

The streets were loud, their whispers sweet,
They promised power, they felt like home.
I traded wisdom for fleeting pride,
Now I wander, cold and alone.

I see you now, your silent tears,
Your prayers unspoken; your hopes denied.
If only I'd listened, if only I'd stayed,
Regret is a flame that burns inside.

Warn the living, call them nearby,
Tell them stories shaped by fear.
The world is ruthless, sharp, unkind,
Hold them close; don't fall behind.

Guide their steps with steady grace,
Be their shield, their safe embrace.
Teach them love before it's late,
A moment's choice can seal their fate.

I am sorry, Mother, I am sorry, Father,
I long for peace, for a life rewound.
Protect the young, fight through the dark,
Save their souls while they're still found.

5

Lost to the Streets

Mothers, fathers, take a stand,
Shield your children from the evil hand.
Whispers lure them in the night,
Promising power, wealth, and might,
But in shadows, danger lies,
Dreams replaced by silent cries.

They recruit our children to sell their drugs,
Trade their futures for fleeting hugs.
Cold streets become their deadly stage,
Hearts corrupted by greed and rage.
Broken homes breed shattered souls,
Chasing fire that devours whole.

In their hands, they place a gun,
Turning boys to men before lives begun.
Pull the trigger for false respect,
Leave behind a life wrecked.
Violence taught in twisted schools,
Where life's currency breaks all rules.

Tell them to kill for protection's sake,
A bitter price no child should take.
Lines are drawn, blood's the ink,
Hope fades faster than we think.
Lives lost beneath the city's glare,
Cold streets show no love, no care.

Mothers, fathers, save your child,
Before the streets turn fierce and wild.
Stand united, build a way,
Guide them toward a brighter day.
Raise your voice, break the chain,
Let no child be lost again.

Hope still flickers in the dark,
Love can heal a wounded heart.
Strengthened homes, a steadfast plan,
Together, we reclaim our land.
Rise with courage, fight the fight,
Save our children from the night.

6

The Silent Struggles: A Verse on Mental Health

In shadows deep, the young hearts cry,
A pain unseen beneath the sky.
Fathers gone, their footsteps fade,
Leaving scars where dreams were made.

Abuse within the walls they call home,
Turns love to fear, and leaves them alone.
The echo of rage, the sting of a hand,
A child adrift in a desolate land.

They sit at the table, yet feel out of place,
A ghost in a family, a forgotten face.
Their laughter drowned by the weight they bear,
Seeking love in a world unfair.

Mental storms rage within their mind,
A maze of pain, no peace to find.
The seeds of despair, sown young and deep,
Steal their joy, even in sleep.

Absence of guidance, a father's embrace,
Leaves hollow spaces time can't replace.
A cycle of anguish, a bitter chain,
Passed through generations, a legacy of pain.

They grow with questions, but answers are few,
A longing for care they never knew.
In silence, they battle, in darkness they fight,
Yearning for warmth, for hope, for light.

Society watches but seldom lends hand,
While these broken spirits barely stand.
Their cries for help, unheard and ignored,
A silent epidemic, hard to afford.

Yet through the despair, resilience grows,
A spark within that often shows.
In art, in words, in actions bold,
They rewrite stories of pain untold.

To mend these hearts, it takes a collective will,

To offer love and teach them skill.
For every lost child deserves to be seen,
A chance to dream, to heal, to glean.
Let us build a world where no child feels alone,
Where every voice is heard, every heart a home.
For mental health, we must take a stand,
Healing young lives with a helping hand.

7

Death on Our Street

Death roams freely on our street,
Do you care? Do you feel the heat?
Our children, lost, killing each other,
A cycle of violence we're trapped within.
Mr. Politician, where is your plan?
Your silence betrays the trust of man.

You bow to pressure, tie police hands,
While blood spills out across these lands.
Stop and search, you cry, it's unfair,
But tell me, do you truly care?
Respect and dignity are all we ask,
For officers sworn to this noble task.

A search today might save a life,
Prevent a blade, avert the strife.
Prison walls won't cage our youth,
If we act with wisdom, seek the truth.
Better a lesson than a cold, hard cell,
Better hope than a living hell.

Parents grieve when the call comes late,
A child lies slain by another's hate.
Yet we complain when help draws near,
Blind to the cost of our misplaced fear.
Justice demands both heart and mind,
A balance of strength and respect combined.

To the leaders, the people, the law we plead,
Stand firm, stand strong, address this need.
Death on our street is a burden we share,
Our children are dying, do you care?
Together we rise, together we fight,
To reclaim our streets and make them right.

Let us stop the cycle before it's too late,
Save lives now, rewrite their fate.
For every child deserves to grow,
To dream, to love, to learn, to know.
Stand up, speak out, no time to delay,
Bring peace to our streets; let's start today.

8

No Winners

No winners when violence reigns,
Broken hearts, enduring pains.
A mother's tears fall like rain,
Her child lost to crime's dark chain.

Behind cold bars or in the ground,
Echoes of grief, a haunting sound.
A knife's swift cut, a gun's loud crack,
Life stolen, there's no turning back.

Communities shattered, spirits torn,
Dreams erased; futures worn.
Silent streets in mourning cry,
As justice hears but can't reply.

Courts decide but can't restore.
A breath, a life, forever more.
Appeals made, but still in vain,
No verdict heals a loved one's pain.

One mistake, one fatal blow,
Regret sinks deep, remorse runs slow.
Choices made in reckless heat.
Leave only loss and sad defeat.

No winners here, just endless strife,
A stolen youth, a wasted life.
Let peace be sown where hope has died,
Before more tears are shed, more lives collide.

9

United We Stand Against Knife Crime

In shadowed streets where fear resides,
Young lives are lost, the pain divides.
A single blade, a fatal scar,
A future stolen, dreams left ajar.
But we must rise, we must unite,
To end this war, to stop this fight.

Each life we save, each path we guide,
Turns tides of sorrow, shifts the tide.
No child should walk in fear alone,
No mother grieve by silent stone.
Through love and care, through hands held tight,
We pave the way from dark to light.

The lessons taught must shape the youth,
To hold to wisdom, walk in truth.
Let schools and homes be voices strong,
To steer our children right from wrong.
For knowledge arms more than a knife,
It grants them hope, it gifts them life.

The law must serve, protect, defend,
But trust must grow for wounds to mend.
Let bridges form, not walls be raised,
So peace may shine where blood once grazed.
A bond of faith in place of dread,
A future built, not filled with red.

To every heart that mourns the slain,
We vow their loss will not be vain.
A nation's duty, bold and true,
To shield its youth, to see them through.
For love unites where hate divides,
And light prevails where hope abides.

So take my hand, stand side by side,
Let courage conquer fear and pride.
No street should echo pain and cries,
No parent weep as promise dies.
Together strong, we break the chain,
And peace shall rise, not fall again.

10

Why Do We Do the Things We Do?

Why do we do the things we do?
Is it because there's no other way,
To get the help we need today?
Begging for bread, though still alive,
Taking to the streets to survive,
A cold bed where hope won't thrive.

Promises made with polished grace,
"People first", a hollow phrase,
Trust dissolves in their deceitful haze.
Their smiles mask greed's intent,
While we drown in unpaid rent,
Dreams shattered, hopes spent.

We scrub their floors from dawn till night,
Labour unseen, denied our rights,
They prosper while we fight our fights.
We ask for justice, our voices soar,
Their response, slam the exit door,
Leaving us poorer than before.

They rise while we fall through the cracks,
We carry burdens on weary backs,
Their wealth grows as compassion lacks.
Empty plates, unpaid dues,
Lives reduced to headline news,
A system rigged for us to lose.

Still, we march, heads held high,
Defying despair, refusing to die,
Chasing dreams no coin can buy.
For dignity can't be taken away,
Our spirits shine through the darkest day,
Fighting still for a better way.

Blood on the Streets of London

Why so much blood on the streets of London?
Shattered lives, dreams left undone.
Youthful faces lost in the night,
Postcode wars dimming future's light.

Why so much hatred, where's the peace?
Violence rising, it never seems to cease.
Over colours, turf, and fleeting pride,
Another soul falls, another mother cried.

Where is the love we used to know?
Hope fades fast where fear does grow.
Communities broken, trust torn apart,
A city in mourning with a heavy heart.

No respect for law, for teacher's voice,
Rebellion speaks loudly, drowning choice.
Discipline's forgotten, guidance ignored,
A silent war waged without a sword.

Where are the fathers, the guiding hands?
Absent in homes, scattered like sands.
Lost generations searching for a way,
Craving direction but led astray.

Rise up, London, break the chain,
Heal the wounds, ease the pain.
Bring back hope, let love increase,
Turn bloodstained streets into paths of peace.

Lost Generation

Where are the leaders, bold and wise,
Guiding young souls toward the skies?
Shadows of purpose fade away,
Leaving the youth to drift astray.

Moral compasses cracked and worn,
Respect for elders tattered, torn.
Voices of wisdom drowned by noise,
Tempted by hollow, fleeting joys.

Parents burdened, stretched too thin,
Battling worlds that cage them in.
Who will teach what's right, what's just,
When trust itself turns into dust?

Schools once sacred, safe, and strong,
Now struggle to right what's gone wrong.
Lessons of life lost in the haze,
Blurred by a world of endless craze.

Media paints dreams dark and wild,
Stealing innocence from each child.
Chasing fame with empty pride,
While hearts grow colder deep inside.

Yet hope still flickers, dim but bright,
A spark ignites in darkest night.
If love, truth, and care survive,
The lost can find their way and thrive.

13

Shattered Streets

In the shadows of broken lanes,
Dreams dissolve like winter rains.
Hope fades in a silent plea,
Lost in the fog of misery.
Shattered streets, cold and bare,
Echo stories of deep despair.

Once proud homes now stand in shame,
Forgotten faces, forgotten names.
Promises broken, futures denied,
Hollow hearts where hope once thrived.
Shattered streets, stained with tears,
Haunted by relentless fears.

Darkened alleys breed deceit,
Whispers of crime fill the street.
Justice sleeps, blind and still,
Prey falls victim to ruthless will.
Shattered streets, marred by sin,
A fight for peace we cannot win.

Children cry through sleepless nights,
Mothers pray beneath dim lights.
Fathers struggle, battles lost,
Dreams shattered at fate's cold cost.
Shattered streets, bruised and torn,
Silent in the face of scorn.

Once there was pride, now there's pain,
Dreams washed out in endless rain.
The past's glory a distant gleam,
Drowned in life's relentless stream.
Shattered streets, hearts confined,
Hope reduced to what we find.

But from ruins, hope might rise,
Through stormy nights and darkened skies.
One kind act, one steady hand,
Could rebuild this battered land.
Shattered streets may heal in time,
When compassion's light begins to shine.

14

Silent Cries

A child's heart breaks in muted tears,
A world of sorrow wrapped in fears.
No gentle touch, no warmth, no light,
Just endless shadows in the night.

Eyes that sparkle hide the ache,
A fragile soul left to break.
Silent battles fought alone,
Love, a dream they've never known.

Scars that hands can never trace,
Pain etched deep behind the face.
A weary spirit worn and torn,
Yearning for a heart reborn.

Neglected voice, unheard plea,
Lost in a world of cruelty.
A tender soul crushed by disdain,
Left to bear unspoken pain.

No arms to hold, no smile to see,
No safe place to simply be.
Hope a whisper, faint and small,
Drowned beneath a loveless call.

Yet through the dark, a flame may glow,
Resilient hearts learn how to grow.
Love withheld but still desired,
Dreams of warmth forever inspired.

15

The Street Speaks

He said, "You don't know me," with fire in his eyes,
Born in the shadows where hope rarely lies.
You judge my hoodie, my slang, my strut,
But never the wounds where the world left a cut.

"You don't know my story," he cried through the night,
The sirens, the hunger, the fear and the fight.
Mama worked double, Dad never came,
So the block raised a boy with no praise, just shame.

They called him a menace, a danger, a threat,
Just numbers and files, they'd rather forget.
But behind every scowl, there's a tear he won't show,
A child of neglect with no safe place to go.

"I walk a hard road," he said with a sigh,
Where friends fade fast and dreams often die.
They label me 'lost', a cause they won't save,
But I am the seed that still dares to be brave.

It don't have to be this way, hear my cry,
I was built for the stars, not just to get by.
I can rise, I can shine, I can build, I can lead,
I'm more than your stats or the hunger I feed.

Be strong, young king, don't let them define,
Your worth by your postcode, your struggle, your grind.
Be positive, stand tall, rewrite your name,
Turn pain into power, and fire into flame.

So tell your story, don't let it be stolen,
Your truth is a weapon, your spirit unbroken.
Be the change that the next one can see,
Not a product of society, but who you choose to be.

16

Hidden Scars

Can't see with the eyes,
But deep wounds remain,
A child carries burdens,
Of sorrow and pain.
Whispers of silence,
A soul left alone,
Heartbeats of anguish,
A chill to the bone.

Bruises don't show,
But the spirit is torn,
Promises shattered,
Dreams left forlorn.
Neglected, forgotten,
A shadow in light,
Fading in darkness,
Consumed by the night.

Behind quiet smiles
Lies a storm untold,
Memories that sting,
And secrets that hold.
Words left unspoken,
Hope dimmed by despair,
A fragile existence
Worn thin by care.

No love to choose,
No hand to extend,
Loneliness lingers,
A never-healed bend.
The past etched in silence,
Invisible chains,
A future uncertain,
Bound by old pains.

Through hollow-eyed stares
And unvoiced cries,
A child battles demons
No one denies.
Scars are well hidden,

The world looks away,
Pretending it's fine,
When nothing's okay.

But still, there's a spark,
Buried deep in the soul,
A flicker of strength
To fight for the whole.
Though wounded and weary,
The spirit can rise,
Casting off shadows,
Reaching for skies.

See beyond faces,
Look through the guise,
Hear silent stories,
Behind distant eyes.
A child with hidden scars
Still dares to dream,
A life beyond sorrow,
A hope unforeseen.

17

Forty Years of Pain

He was only a child, so small and frail,
In a house where love and hate prevailed.
Beaten, broken, cast aside,
By those meant to love, who only lied.

In public, smiles were forced in place,
But hidden bruises left no trace.
No one knew the storms he faced,
A shattered soul, a life disgraced.

Pain carved deep into his heart,
From family's scorn, torn apart.
Branded fatherless, unwanted, alone,
A child seeking warmth in a world of stone.

Despair whispered, "There's no escape,"
Darkness wrapped him in its cape.
Suicide seemed the only door,
But fate refused and gave him more.

God intervened with a silent hand,
Breathing life into a broken man.
From the edge, he rose anew,
Scarred but strong, steady, and true.

Now a father with love to spare,
His children shielded with utmost care.
His past a lesson, his soul refined,
He loves fiercely, with heart and mind.

Forty years of sorrow, pain, and strife,
Transformed through grace into a life.
A protector, a guide, steadfast and strong,
His legacy: love that lasts lifelong.

18

Rise Above

In a world consumed by endless strife,
Where hate and greed shape much of life,
The heart that dares to stand apart,
Becomes a beacon, strong and smart.

Amidst the storms that blind the soul,
Hold kindness firmly as your goal.
Let honesty and truth take lead,
Plant love's pure seed in word and deed.

Temptations lure with fleeting gain,
False riches built on others' pain.
Resist the call of selfish schemes,
Stay true to hope, to higher dreams.

The world may try to dim your light,
But courage turns the darkest night.
Integrity, your guiding flame,
A force no shadow can defame.

Though cruelty reigns in many hearts,
Your mercy sets you worlds apart.
Through every trial, rise anew,
Let compassion define you.

For in the battle for the soul,
The truest victory is control,
Of self, of love, of what we give.
Through grace and truth, we rise… we live.

19

Never Give Up

When shadows loom and hopes decline,
Stand firm, let your spirit shine.
It's better to fall while reaching high,
Then never to leap, fearing the sky.

When storms rage fierce and paths seem blocked,
Remember, every clock is reset when it's stopped.
A closed door's echo is not defeat,
It's destiny calling from the street.

Rise from failure, wipe each tear,
Let courage drown out every fear.
What's lost today might light your way,
Guiding you toward a brighter day.

The journey's long, the climb is steep,
But dreams are sown where faith runs deep.
Push through the dark, pursue your quest,
Persistence carves the path to success.

When all seems gone and doubts intrude,
Recall your strength, your fortitude.
Each setback births a chance anew,
A brighter world is waiting for you.

20

Child Abuse Knows No Boundaries

In shadows where silence reigns,
In broken homes and tear-stained lanes,
A child's cry echoes through the night,
Begging for love, longing for light.

Bruises fade, but memories stay,
Silent screams won't drift away.
Trust shattered, innocence lost,
A heavy burden, a tragic cost.

No face, no race, no creed confined,
Abuse strikes without a sign.
Rich or poor, near or far,
Pain leaves an everlasting scar.

A gentle word, a safe embrace,
Can mend a soul and heal disgrace.
Love's light breaks through the dark,
Restoring hope, igniting a spark.

Stand as guardians, fierce and strong,
Right the grievous, fight the wrong.
Shield the weak, defend their dreams,
Be the refuge from life's schemes.

For every child deserves to grow
With peace, with joy, with hearts aglow.
Their rights are sacred, pure, divine.
Let justice speak, let love shine.

21

What Kind of World?

What kind of world are we living in,
Where hearts grow cold, and compassion wears thin?
Mothers weep while children cry,
Yet promises of hope fade and die.

No love, no care for the battle-worn,
Veterans left broken, forgotten, and torn.
They fought for peace, yet find none nearby,
A life of struggle, wrapped in fear.

We spend billions on wars afar,
Fuelling fire, leaving scars.
While streets overflow with homeless souls,
No home, no shelter, no worthy goals.

Basic needs denied, dreams confined,
Justice lost in greed's cruel bind.
Where is mercy? Where is grace?
Human dignity erased without a trace.

Rise, awaken, hear their plea,
End this cycle; set them free.
Build with kindness, not with hate,
Change this world before it's too late.

22

Our Children

In the cradle of innocence, our children dwell,
Our guardianship, a story we must tell.
With tender hearts and watchful eyes,
We shield them from darkness, under azure skies.

Their laughter, a melody, pure and bright,
In their joy, we find our guiding light.
Through fields of dreams, they dance and play,
We vow to protect them, come what may.

In a world of shadows, we stand tall,
Against harm's reach, a protective wall.
With courage forged in love's embrace,
We shield our children, in every space.

For every tear, a fortress we build,
In their presence, our purpose fulfilled.
With every breath, a promise we keep,
To guard their innocence, in slumber deep.

23

Freedom of Speech

In shadows thick, the truth is bound,
Where silence echoes, none profound.
A right once bright, now faint, and weak,
Freedom of speech, no more we speak.

In a world of walls, where censors reign,
Our thoughts confined; our voices strained.
Privilege for few, the chosen high,
While others mute beneath the sky.

You preach of rights, of liberty's flame,
Yet shun the voices that curse your name.
Democracy, a hollow creed,
When fear suppresses every need.

Our words, like whispers in the storm,
Are lost, reshaped, to fit the norm.
Still, we resist, defy the night,
For truth demands its sacred light.

Though chains may bind, though cells may close,
A spark within forever glows.
No bars can hold what minds conceive,
For speech, once free, will never leave.

24

No Hopes, No Dream

No hopes, no dream, a silent cry,
Beneath the stars, unanswered why,
Promises fade like clouds in the sky,
Leaving the broken to struggle and try.

The streets are harsh, cold, and bare,
Ambition crushed by life's despair,
Shattered hopes float in the air,
A cycle of loss too cruel to bear.

Through hollow nights and restless days,
Youth wander lost in life's dark maze,
Searching for light in deceitful haze,
Seeking purpose through endless delays.

Dreams deferred, yet spirits ignite,
Resistance born from endless fight,
Hope rekindled in darkest night,
Determined hearts reclaim their right.

They stand as one, strong and bold,
Stories of pain yet untold,
Forging futures from steel and gold,
Breaking free from oppression's hold.

With every fall, they learn to rise,
Piercing through deceitful lies,
Building dreams beneath boundless skies,
Chasing hope that never dies.

No hopes, no dream, once a refrain,
But now they rise through strife and pain,
Crafting a world where love shall reign,
A future redeemed from endless chain.

25

Silent Steps

In a house of shattered dreams, they cried,
A tender soul, hope denied.
Whispers of pain in the dead of night,
Silent battles fought out of sight.

A touch meant for comfort turned cold,
Love replaced by a grip too bold.
Fragile wings crushed by hate,
Locked behind a merciless gate.

The street beckoned with hollow embrace,
A refuge found in a ruthless place.
Among shadows, the child would roam,
Searching for safety, far from home.

Criminal hands offered false relief,
Trading innocence for fleeting peace.
Trust broken beyond repair,
A child lost in a world unfair.

Memories linger, sharp as knives,
Carving wounds that scar their lives.
No one sees the soul that pleads,
Buried beneath society's weeds.

Yet in the dark, a spark remains,
A will to rise despite the chains.
For even in the harshest strife,
Hope can bloom and reclaim life.

26

Having Seeds of Hope

To sow a dream in youthful hands,
Is casting hope across life's sands.
A spark ignites where shadows lie,
A flame that dares to touch the sky.

Through storms of doubt and fear's cold breath,
The seed of hope defies near-death.
Its roots dig deep through rock and clay,
Determined still to find its way.

Each trial faced, each battle won,
Strengthens the stem beneath the sun.
Its leaves unfurl with lessons learned,
From pain endured and bridges burned.

And when its blossom graces dawn,
New seeds of hope are swiftly drawn.
They scatter wide on winds of grace,
Transforming hearts in every place.

One tender sprout can break the stone,
Revive lost dreams long left alone.
Its power vast, its reach untold,
A single hope is wealth of gold.

So, plant with care, with love, with might,
A future built on guiding light.
For seeds of hope, though small they seem,
Hold endless worlds within their dream.

27

A Child's Truth

He stood there, only ten years old,
Eyes wide with stories, untold yet bold.
"The only way back to my birthland's gate,
Is if most of my family meets a cruel fate."

Ninety-five percent gone, dead or confined,
A reality etched deep in his young mind.
A boy robbed of dreams, a future unclear,
His voice steady yet trembling with fear.

But Moore never cared, he turned away,
Moved the date, left them as prey.
No warning given, no shield held tight,
Abandoned to shadows in the dead of night.

I stood firm when no one would,
Did what human decency says I should.
Life comes first, before profit or pride,
A truth I carry, deep inside.

Moore, hear this, wealth can return,
But lost dignity leaves souls to burn.
Human worth isn't a stock to trade,
It's the light in the darkness, never to fade.

So, remember this child, his plea, his face,
And know that no fortune can ever replace.
A heart that protects, a soul that defends,
For life's true measure is how it ends.

28

The Power Within

Let no one tell you, "You can't achieve your goal,"
The fire you need is born within your soul.
Each doubt they cast is just a test to face,
With courage strong, you'll find your rightful place.

Follow your dream, step by step, don't stray,
Even the tallest mountains wear away.
The path is steep, the nights may feel too long,
But faith and focus keep the spirit strong.

You can, you can, believe it when you say,
Success will meet you if you don't delay.
Your voice, your light, your gift, let them all rise,
And reach beyond the limits others prize.

So keep believing, though storms may roar,
You're built for more than what you've done before.
No wall too high, no sea too wide to cross,
When driven by belief, you count no loss.

Work hard, it won't be easy, that is true,
But greatness only comes to those who do.
Endure the trial, embrace the sweat and strain,
And let your purpose justify the pain.

It will be worth its sacrifice in time,
Your name engraved in destiny's design.
Stand tall, press on, let willpower lead the way,
The dawn is yours, and this your breaking day.

29

Never Let the Street Think for You

Never let the street think for you,
Its whispers deceive, its path untrue.
Your mind's a forge of infinite might,
Shape your world, pursue the light.

The streets may lure with fleeting gains,
Tempting hearts with hollow chains.
But dreams are forged by inner fire,
Not by shadows that conspire.

Think for yourself, rise above,
Feed your soul with hope and love.
Your destiny's carved by what you do,
Not by the crowds that follow through.

Let no one shatter your belief,
Or fill your heart with doubt or grief.
Stand firm when storms assail your way,
The dawn will break a brighter day.

Reject the lies that dim your flame,
Walk with purpose, not for fame.
Your journey's yours, unique, profound,
Let wisdom guide where steps are bound.

So, listen close, hear your call,
Stand upright, fearless, and tall.
The power within can set you free,
Master your mind, claim victory.

30

Forgotten Soldiers

They marched for us through fire and sand,
With rifle clenched in trembling hand.
For flag and freedom, they stood tall,
Watched their brothers rise, and watched them fall.
But now they sleep on concrete stone,
A war hero turned ghost, alone.

The battle's done, or so they say,
But in their mind, it plays each day.
PTSD, a silent scream,
A shadow stalking every dream.
You see a man with tattered pride,
Not all wounds bleed from the outside.

They fought for country, fought for us,
For every right we now hold true.
You raise your glass, you sing your song,
But can't spare change when they walk wrong.
You cheer for freedom, decked in red,
While they find bins to earn their bread.

The medals rust in worn-out coats,
Their thanks? A shrug, some pity notes.
You decorate the streets with lights,
But not one shelter warms their nights.
You make it merry, dance and dine,
As if this silence isn't theirs.

They came back home to find no peace,
No safety, care, nor sweet release.
This battle now is just to eat,
To dodge the cold and guard their feet.
They trained them well to brave the fight,
But not to beg beneath a light.

So light your trees, pretend you care,
Wave flags as if they're truly there.
But know this pain they choose to blind
Still haunts the hearts they left behind.
They fought for all that you believe,
But came back only to grieve.

31

Word is Power

For all my childhood life,
I heard the echoes, sharp like a knife,
"Good for nothing, a hopeless cause,"
Words like chains, enforcing pause.

But I refused to be confined,
Shut out their doubts from my mind.
Their harsh predictions, I cast aside,
Fuelling the fire that burned inside.

A voice within, steady and strong,
Whispered to me all along:
"You are worthy, you belong,
Rise above; prove them wrong."

I'm crafted with purpose, born from grace,
A child of God, running the race.
Destined for heights they cannot see,
Their words can't define my destiny.

Every setback became my fuel,
Their judgment, a broken tool.
I built with courage, brick by brick,
Turned their curses into a trick.

Word is power, truth and lies,
It builds, destroys, lifts, or denies.
I choose belief, I choose my voice,
I shape my life, my rightful choice.

32

Rise Above

I might be brought up in a broken home,
Where warmth was scarce and love unknown.
I might be raised where pennies were few,
With empty plates and hunger that grew.

My parents might never have seen a college door,
Struggling through life, weary and poor.
Nights may have passed with no food to share,
Whispers of hope dissolved in despair.

I might have lived in a fostered place,
Longing for family, comfort, and grace.
A name on a file, a child in need,
Searching for roots, a future to lead.

But that doesn't mean I'm doomed to fall,
I'm not the weakest, I stand tall.
Dreams still burn in my hopeful eyes,
I'll carve my path beneath open skies.

I can break the chains of poverty's snare,
Rewrite my story with courage and care.
The streets won't claim the life in me,
I'm destined for more than what they see.

The sky is vast, and I'll rise high,
No limit will cage my will to try.
Through storms and struggle, I will soar,
A future of promise forever in store.

33

I Will Decide My Own Destiny

I will decide my own destiny, not you,
With my dreams clear, my path in view.
I'll go to school, learn a trade,
Or strive in university where futures are made.
My fate's my own, I'll rise and be true.

I'll gain an education, strong and bright,
A beacon to guide me through the night.
With knowledge as my armor, wisdom my sword,
I'll build a future I can afford,
A life of purpose, lit with light.

What I won't do is take your guns,
Be your assassin, or harm someone.
I won't sell your drugs, destroy my name,
Or be a menace lost in shame.
This is my vow; I'll be no one's pawn.

I'll stand tall with dignity and pride,
Through storms and struggles, I won't hide.
For my family I'll shine, for myself I'll glow,
Through hard work and honour, the seeds I'll sow,
With truth and courage as my guide.

I'll make them proud; I'll make me proud,
Rise above the noise, stand out in the crowd.
No shortcuts, no lies, no path of strife,
I'll walk the road of an honest life,
Building a legacy, noble and loud.

So I say no to crime and violence today,
No to the darkness that leads hearts astray.
With hope in my heart and fire in my soul,
I'll conquer the world and achieve my goal.
This is my destiny, my chosen way.

34

Letting Go

Violence against women is never right,
No excuse can shroud that blight.
Love isn't chains that bind or break,
It's the freedom two souls partake.

Letting go isn't giving in,
It's not defeat, nor mortal sin.
It's seeing clearly through love's haze,
When paths diverge in life's vast maze.

Sometimes love means stepping back,
Releasing dreams you used to track.
Not from failure, fear, or spite,
But for healing in the heart's own light.

Two souls may touch but not entwine,
Their destinies in different lines.
No blame, no hate, just truth laid bare,
A farewell spoken with silent care.

Trust in the future's unseen grace,
That peace will find its rightful place.
Growth comes when we learn to be,
Both rooted strong and flying free.

Love doesn't fade when you let go,
It transforms, reshapes, and flows.
Through memories held, through lessons learned,
Through quiet strength in hearts that yearned.

So, part with kindness, let pain cease,
Release with courage, find your peace.
Love's true gift is to set free,
What's meant will bloom in destiny.

35

9/11

A day in history I will never forget, 9/11
A day in my lifetime I will never forget, 9/11
I will never forget, 9/11
So many died by the hands of people who hate our way of life.

They took our families, friends,
colleagues and our loved ones.
They took them all on 9/11

Grieving mothers, fathers, brothers, sisters, grandparents,
cousins, aunts, sons, friends, and daughters,
everyone who lost a loved one on 9/11,
We feel your pain.

We will heal together,
But we will never forget,
We will cry together,
But we will never forget.

The pain of the families of 9/11
The sacrifices of the emergency services on 9/11
Will never be forgotten.

And those who hate our way of life,
Who preach violence, hate, and terror,
They will never win.

36

Shattered Streets, Silent Fears

The street once a haven, now drenched in despair,
Where shadows linger and danger is near.
The elders walk with hesitant stride,
In a country they built with love and pride.
Why must their twilight be clouded with dread,
In fear of the night, of the path they tread.

Hands that tilled the soil and paved the way,
Now tremble in fear of the predator's sway.
Robbed of their peace, their dignity torn,
In a nation their sacrifices adorn.
They gave us their years, their strength, their all,
Yet find no comfort as darkness falls.

Why should the streets echo cries of alarm,
When once they resounded with laughter's charm?
The elderly shuffle, afraid to meet eyes,
Haunted by whispers of violence and lies.
The home they defended now turns away,
Their golden years tarnished, their hope in decay.

And where are the leaders, the voices of power,
In this broken and perilous hour?
Do they see the plight, the pain, the despair,
Of a generation left gasping for air?
What laws have they written, what care have they shown,
For the hands that built the streets they own?

Oh, country of wealth, of progress and might,
Why let your elders fade into the night?
Their wisdom unheeded, their struggles ignored,
As crime and neglect cut deeper than swords.
Can justice awaken, can compassion arise,
To heal the wounds beneath the skies?

Let us reclaim these streets with grace,
Restore the safety, the love, the embrace.
For the elders who gave us all that we know,
Let their twilight in peace and security glow.
A nation is judged by how it defends,
The lives of its weakest, until the very end.

37

Youth Poverty, a Cry for Help

Amidst the city's endless beat,
Young souls in poverty, their fate they meet.
On the streets, they find their home,
No place to call their very own.

Hungry eyes and ragged clothes they wear,
No shoes to shield them from life's despair.
In a world so cruel and incomplete,
These young hearts, society's harsh defeat.

Food banks struggle, shelves grow bare,
While we send billions to lands in warfare.
Can't we turn to our own in need,
Before we plant more of war's poisonous seed?

Tears fall from my eyes like rain,
Seeing youth's dreams go down the drain.
Is there a future for the poor and sore,
When help and compassion we choose to ignore?

Let's lend a hand, find a way to care,
For the young in poverty, life's burden to bear.
Together we can change the score,
A future of hope, compassion in store.

38

Kindness

In a world where kindness should reign,
No one above, no one to disdain.
Treat others as you wish to be,
Respect and kindness set us free.

Costless gestures, yet treasures untold,
In the heart of respect, compassion unfolds.
Why choose meanness, why be unkind,
When harmony and warmth are what we find?

A gentle word can heal a soul,
A caring act can make one whole.
Each little deed, a ripple of care,
A brighter world for all to share.

Kindness does not ask for fame,
It seeks no glory, no loud acclaim.
Its strength is quiet, yet deeply profound,
A force that lifts and knows no bound.

In giving, we find a gift in return,
A spark of joy, a lesson to learn.
A life enriched by love's embrace,
A kinder heart, a better place.

So let us sow these seeds each day,
In every action, in every way.
For kindness builds a bridge to peace,
And brings the world a sweet release.

39

Our Heroes Live

In the shadows of despair, they rise anew,
Defiant spirits, steadfast and true.
Bound by chains, yet their dreams take flight,
Illuminating darkness with eternal light.
Through pain and loss, their courage grows,
Their silent strength, a force that flows.

When justice falters, and hope seems frail,
Their voices echo, a resounding tale.
They build the bridges where others divide,
Carving paths where heroes reside.
Their sacrifices forge futures bright,
Guiding the lost toward the light.

Through blood-soaked soil, their seeds are sown,
Their legacies rooted; their greatness known.
Not for glory, nor fleeting fame,
But for the promise that justice remains.
Each act of valour, each word they give,
Proclaims the truth: our heroes live.

Their wisdom whispers through winds that roar,
In every battle, they stand once more.
Immortal souls, in history's scroll,
Unyielding hearts, unbroken whole.
Though time may weather the stones they mark,
Their deeds endure, a blazing spark.

For heroes dwell where courage reigns,
In hearts unbowed by worldly chains.
They teach us strength, to rise and fight,
To hold the torch and guard the light.
In every struggle, their spirits thrive,
Unseen, but steadfast, our heroes live.

So let us honour their righteous stand,
The architects of a freer land.
Their voices echo through distant skies,
A call to action, where hope lies.
In unity's embrace, their dreams we give,
Eternal truth, our heroes live.

40

Justice Unyielding

Justice must never bow to race,
Nor yield its strength to power's embrace.
No throne, no crown, no fleeting name,
Can tilt the scales or dim its flame.

Not politics with cunning hand,
Should bend its will or take command.
For justice lives, unchained, untamed,
By fleeting games where truth is blamed.

Colour cannot define the way,
That justice strides, both night and day.
Its eyes are blind, its heart is pure,
Through every trial, it must endure.

Class holds no sway, no special key,
To twist its path or make it see,
Through lenses false, of greed or pride,
Justice must walk on truth's clear side.

A shield for those whom life denies,
A sword for truth when darkness lies.
Equality must be its creed,
To lift the low and check the greed.

So let it stand, upright, unbowed,
No whispers soft or threats aloud
Can shake the voice of truth's decree,
For justice guards humanity.

41

Where Are They Now?

What's wrong, why you look so sad?
Eyes once bright, now worn and bad,
They pushed and pushed 'til you gave in,
Said you were family, said you were kin.
A brother in arms, they called you strong,
Promised the streets where you belong,
But every word they spoke was wrong.

They lied to you with twisted charm,
Used your pain to cause more harm.
You held the blade, you took the fall,
While they just vanished past the wall.
You did the deeds they dared not show,
Now it's your name the records know,
Trapped in a life you didn't grow.

They gave you colours, not a cause,
They gave you cheers, then cold applause.
Said loyalty was blood and pride,
But bled you dry, then stepped aside.
No honour in the path you tread,
Just echoes of the things they said,
And faces blurred, long since they fled.

Now you're standing before the judge,
Heavy silence, no one to nudge.
Twenty-five to life they say,
Your dreams now locked and cast away.
Where are the boys who had your back?
They're ghosts along a one-way track,
Not one showed up to face the facts.

You're on your own in a concrete room,
Living shadows, breathing gloom.
A number now, not someone's son,
Paying dues for what they've done.
Stripped of hope, of nights and days,
You count regrets in endless ways,
But freedom's price no gang repays.

Mama cried but didn't speak,
Her strength now dim, her soul feels weak.
She begged you once to walk away,
But pride and pressure made you stay.
She lights a candle, says a prayer,
Still wishing you were never there,
Caught in a lie, beyond repair.

Yet even here, behind these bars,
You still can reach beyond the scars.
This isn't where your story ends,
There's still a path to make amends.
Though they betrayed you, sold your trust,
You rise again from broken dust,
To find new truth, because you must.

42

Think Before You Act

In the heat of rage, when tempers rise,
When pride and ego wear a bold disguise,
Pause a moment, breathe in deep,
The seeds you sow are yours to reap.

A choice once made, a path once trod,
Can steal your peace and anger God.
So weigh your steps, let wisdom guide,
For foolish hearts in prison reside.

Think before you raise your hand,
Before you strike, before you stand
On ground that leads to deep regret,
A road of pain you won't forget.

That blade, that gun, that flash of hate,
Can seal another person's fate.
And once it's done, no words undo
The haunting eyes that once looked through.

You'll wear the guilt, the silent scream,
In every night, in every dream.
No freedom comes with blood-stained pride,
Just shackled thoughts you cannot hide.

So think before you cross the line,
Before you trade your soul for time.
A single act, a lifetime lost,
Decisions come, but oh, the cost.

43

God is the Anchor

No matter the storm you face, my brother,
When skies turn dark and shadows smother,
Stand firm though waves rise bold and strong,
The night may be fierce, but it won't last long.
For in the tempest's loudest roar,
God is the anchor at your core.

The winds may howl, the currents sway,
And doubt may try to steal your way,
But do not fear, don't lose your ground,
There's power in the prayers unbound.
Your tears are not cried out in vain,
Through trials, God will break the chain.

Don't give up, for you're not alone,
Many are walking paths unknown.
Their silent battles mirror yours,
Their dreams held behind unseen doors.
Together we march, though burdens weigh,
Hope is the torch that lights our way.

Strength comes not from might or pride,
But from the faith you hold inside.
Kneel in the storm, and you shall rise,
With fire of purpose in your eyes.
Your scars will tell the tale you own,
Of how the seed of faith was sown.

Victory whispers through the pain,
A gentle voice like healing rain.
It tells of dawn beyond the night,
Of wrongs made right, of dark turned light.
So press on, brother, don't retreat,
Each trial brings your crown complete.

So let the storm break, let it cry,
Let questions rise and time pass by.
God holds the ship and charts your course,
With grace your sail and love your force.
Though oceans rage and mountains groan,
The anchor holds. You're not alone.

44

What More Can You Take?

What more can you take, when I've nothing left to give?
My time, like rivers, flowed through the cracks of how you live.
My strength was yours in silence, in the battles you ignored,
Yet here you stand demanding, with your eyes a sharpened sword.
Do you not see the emptiness, the hollow in my core?

I gave my soul in whispers, in the quiet midnight cries,
Held your storms within my chest, wore your truths and your lies.
I stood when I was breaking, built your world from pieces torn,
Now you want the ashes, of a heart already worn.
What more do you require, from bones stripped to the floor?

My hands once held the sunrise just to place it at your feet,
My voice a song of solace, even when I knew defeat.
I bled in noble silence, so your shadows wouldn't grow,
And still you point with hunger, as if you didn't know,
I've fed you with my lifeblood till there's nothing left in store.

Each moment I surrendered was a prayer you never heard,
Yet I remained unwavering, kept my promise, kept my word.
You dined upon my mercy, you drank my quiet pain,
While I danced beneath your thunder, kissed your ever-falling rain.
Was I not enough, though I gave more than ever before?

So now I ask in stillness, in the echo of the fall,
What more can you take, when I have given you my all?
No more tears to water you, no more roots to hold this tree,
Just the shell of what I was, and the ghost of loyalty.
Take the silence, if it speaks louder than my call.

45

Would You Treat Me the Same?

If I was Black or if I was White,
Would your gaze soften, or sharpen in spite?
Would your smile stretch or your silence remain?
Would the colour I wear shape your disdain?
Do I need to explain the skin that I'm in,
Or prove to your eyes that my worth lies within?

If I was born where the sun kisses sand,
Or crossed many seas to stand in this land,
Would you see me as equal, or label my name,
A stranger, a threat, should I carry that shame?
Would you hold out a hand or build up a wall,
When all that I ask is a place for us all?

If I was White, would your welcome be wide?
Would doors open quicker, would truth choose my side?
Would justice be blind or blink in my case,
Would you look past the skin and just see the face?
Or is fairness a mirror that shifts with the light,
Bending the rules when the shade isn't right?

What if my roots ran Asian and deep,
Would I be judged by the language I keep?
Would culture and spice make me foreign to you,
Or would you embrace all the colours and hues?
Would accents offend or stories inspire,
Would my heritage raise you or fuel your fire?

If I hailed from islands where palm trees sway,
Would you mock my tone or hear what I say?
Would the rhythm I bring be welcome here,
Or lost in a system that feeds on fear?
From Kingston to Port of Spain, I bleed
The same red as you, don't let hate lead.

Treat people the way you'd wish for your own,
With kindness and love, not coldness or stone.
No matter the shade, the place, or the name,
We all seek respect, and we all feel pain.
So break down the walls and silence the blame,
Let justice be colourless, and treat me the same.

46

Bridging the Gap

In corners where the young hearts roam,
And streets too often steal their home,
Let uniforms not bring dismay,
But guide the youth to brighter day.
With clubs where trust and hope begin,
The change we seek can grow within.

A place where badges speak with care,
Not just enforce but truly share,
Where laughter lives and dreams arise,
Beneath the same wide London skies.
A mentor's voice, a steady hand,
Can help a troubled soul to stand.

Through music, sports, and open talk,
Alongside those who daily walk
The beat through fear and shattered dreams,
Can come new bonds and brighter themes.
No longer strangers, side by side,
In unity, let trust abide.

A space where wrong turns find redress,
Where hope is worn like Sunday dress,
Where youth are shown a better way,
To shape tomorrow from today.
When coppers coach and captains lead,
We plant the roots of noble seed.

Beyond the sirens and the chase,
Let young ones see a human face.
A name, a story, strength, and grace,
Not judgment, but a warm embrace.
These clubs can break the silence loud,
And lift our children from the crowd.

Let every borough, block, and lane,
Be touched by purpose, not by pain.
With uniforms who serve and strive
To keep young dreams not just alive,
But thriving through each noble deed,
A true response to urgent need.

So let us build, with hearts sincere,
These clubs where youth and law draw near.
From fear to faith, from doubt to trust,
We mend the bond that time has crushed.
With every game, each spoken word,
A future fairer will be heard.

47

United We Stand to Save Our Youths

In streets once filled with childhood games,
Now echo cries and mourned-out names,
Where blades have stolen dreams away,
We must rise up, no more delay.
This fight is ours, both great and small,
To save our youth, to break the fall.

No postcode, faith, or skin defines
The pain inflicted by these crimes.
A mother's tears, a father's plea,
It touches all, not just a few.
So let us drop our walls of pride,
And walk as one, all side by side.

The youth cry out for love and hope,
Not warnings etched in flowers and smoke.
Let mentors rise, let leaders speak,
Let silence fall where weapons sneak.
Each hand we lend, each ear we lend,
Can shape a path, can help amend.

Schools and homes and hearts must be
The frontline in this unity.
Police alone can't mend the seams,
It takes a nation's shared belief.
In every heart a light must burn,
For every child, it is their turn.

So, stand with courage, firm and proud,
Let every voice be fierce and loud.
This war is won not through the sword,
But care, and trust, and healing words.
For every life holds worth untold,
A story waiting to unfold.

Together now, no turning back,
Let's walk the peace, not fear the track.
The future's written in our choice,
So rise as one, and raise your voice.
United, bold, we'll lead the way,
A safer dawn, a brighter day.

48

If We Fail Them Today

If we fail to shield the dreams they hold,
To guide their hearts through streets grown cold,
Then we, as stewards, bear the cost,
Of every bright tomorrow lost.
The nation falls where hope declines,
Its future blurred in broken lines.

Too many blades have pierced our trust,
Turned playgrounds into fields of dust.
We must not wait till cries grow loud,
Or youth lie silent in a shroud.
Let knowledge be the shield we raise,
To lead them through these shadowed days.

Let classrooms teach more than the test,
But how to lead, forgive, and bless.
Let lessons shine on right and wrong,
And make the weak feel brave and strong.
For every life that we uplift,
Becomes the nation's truest gift.

Bridge the gaps with hands outstretched,
Let no child feel alone, detached.
Police and kin must walk as one,
Till fear and judgment are undone.
Community must light the flame,
And teach our youth they're not to blame.

Replace the knives with pens and dreams,
With songs of peace and hopeful themes.
Teach love instead of vengeful pride,
And let no pain in silence hide.
The world they build begins with this,
A chance to rise, to heal, to miss.

So rise, O nation, take your stand,
With open hearts and helping hands.
The time is now to guide their flight,
From darkest paths into the light.
For if we fail our youth today,
We throw our own tomorrow away.

49

The Light We Pass On

In streets where silence hides the cries,
And broken dreams fill tender eyes,
A mentor's voice, both firm and kind,
Can heal the wounds that scar the mind.
A hand to hold, a path made clear,
To walk in hope, not dwell in fear.

When youth stand lost at life's divide,
Between the dark and truth denied,
A guiding soul can plant the seed,
Of purpose, peace, and noble deed.
For in each heart, a flame can rise,
When shown the world through wiser eyes.

Let parents lift this sacred flame,
Encouraging mentors, proud in name,
Who teach that love can still disarm,
A world grown numb to pain and harm.
Their presence shapes what futures see,
And breaks the chains of misery.

Each story shared, each lesson taught,
Becomes a shield, a calming thought.
Against the blade, against the crime,
We offer strength, not jail or time.
A voice of reason, strong yet free,
Speaks louder than hostility.

Communities must play their part,
With open arms and open heart.
To build a world where youth can grow,
And see the light they're meant to know.
Where knives are left, and dreams are drawn,
On canvases of brighter dawns.

So let us guide, uplift, invest,
In every soul who's lost, oppressed.
For violence fades where love takes lead,
And mentors plant the truest seed.
In unity, we rise above,
To shape a life of peace and love.

50

Where is Our Greatness?

Where is our greatness, the Britain of old,
A nation of courage, of hearts strong and bold?
We once stood for justice, for honour, for peace,
Now all that was golden has started to cease.

The love and the kindness we gave with such grace,
To strangers and neighbours, no matter their race.
We opened our arms to the tired and poor,
But now we build walls, and we bolt up the door.

Our children once dreamt with stars in their eyes,
Now hope disappears beneath grey, silent skies.
We speak without mercy, we judge with such speed,
And trample the fragile, ignore those in need.

Where once we were noble, now power corrupts,
The truth is distorted, and honour disrupts.
The streets echo silence where laughter once played,
And memories of glory begin to fade.

We fed the hungry, we cared for the weak,
Now hearts have grown bitter, and tongues seldom speak.
No unity left, just anger and greed,
No balm for the broken, no answer to plead.

O Britain, awake! Reclaim your lost soul,
Let compassion and truth again be our goal.
Rise from this slumber, restore what was right,
Be the beacon once more, and shine through the night.

51

Our Everyday Heroes

In shadows cast by city light, they rise,
With quiet strength and watchful eyes.
They walk the streets, they bear the load,
Our everyday heroes, brave and bold.
They do not seek the spotlight's gleam,
Yet stand as pillars of our dream,
To live in peace, to heal, to grow,
They serve with heart, and this we know.

True heroes stand not for fame,
But for the lives they seek to claim
From danger's grip, from fate's cruel tide,
With courage fierce, and arms open wide.
Through sleepless nights and endless days,
They walk compassion's rugged ways,
No cape upon their backs you'll see,
Yet they are strong as one can be.

The police patrol both night and day,
To keep the lurking threat at bay.
They run toward what we all flee,
To hold the line for you and me.
In harm's way they stand so firm,
Ensuring justice takes its turn.
With every risk that they embrace,
They wear pure courage on their face.

The firefighters, flames defy,
Charging into smoke-filled sky.
When walls collapse and sirens cry,
They'll carry hope where others die.
They do not flinch, they do not run,
Their work is never truly done.
With every blaze they strive to tame,
They earn their place in honour's name.

Nurses and doctors, healers all,
Answering each frantic call.
With weary hands and steadfast grace,
They ease the pain, they set the pace.
Through pandemics, wounds, and endless strife,

They breathe their strength into new life.
A touch, a word, a silent tear,
Their love is felt when hope draws near.

Care workers, binmen, in the dawn,
Still working when the world moves on.
They keep us fed, they keep us clean,
Their efforts felt but rarely seen.
They lift, they wipe, they smile, they serve,
With every ounce of strength and nerve.
The jobs unseen, the hearts so wide,
True greatness does not always hide.

Social workers face the storm,
To keep the fragile safe and warm.
They hear the cries behind closed doors,
They fight for rights, for just, for more.
With every case, with every plea,
They guard our future silently.
No easy task, no thanks enough,
Their path is steep, their journey tough.

So here's a salute to all you do,
To every silent warrior true.
Your names may not be etched in stone,
But still your legacy is known.
In every act of care and fight,
You bring us hope, you shine your light.
Our everyday heroes, through and through,
We see you, love you, honour you.

52

The Weight He Bears

At twelve years old, he walks alone,
Through broken streets he once called home.
His father slain, his brother too,
A shattered world, no guiding clue.
His mother weeps with empty hands,
No work, no aid, no helping plans.

He holds his brother, frail and small,
While hunger echoes through the hall.
No counsellor, no listening ear,
No friendly voice to draw him near.
He bites his lips and hides his cries,
A boy with manhood in his eyes.

The nights are long, the days are cold,
His heart is heavy, far too old.
The silence screams, the pain runs deep,
No place to dream, no chance to sleep.
And in the dark, he starts to think,
That crime might be his only link.

A stolen gun, a loaded fate,
He walks the path he starts to hate.
He sees the gangs, he hears their lies,
A desperate hope beneath the skies.
But deep within, he feels the weight,
A life of fear, a life of hate.

Until one day, a stranger came,
Not seeking praise, not chasing fame.
With food in hand and kindness shown,
He touched a heart long turned to stone.
He offered help, he offered grace,
He brought back light to that dark place.

A job for Mum, some shoes to wear,
A school that showed the boy they care.
He learned to read, he learned to dream,
A future flowing like a stream.
And all it took, a heart aware,
To simply love, to truly care.